APPLYING AI & MACHINE LEARNING TO SOLVE NIGERIA'S UNIQUE CHALLENGES

Tobi Kabir Yusuf

TABLE OF CONTENTS

PREFACE

Nigeria, a nation blessed with immense natural and human resources, is simultaneously burdened with challenges that seem insurmountable at times. Despite being Africa's largest economy, Nigeria faces significant hurdles, ranging from economic instability to a fragile healthcare system, from educational inequality to insufficient infrastructure, and from governance issues to the persistent threat of insecurity. These challenges are deeply rooted in the country's complex socio-political environment, affecting the everyday lives of millions of Nigerians. Yet, amidst these difficulties lies an incredible opportunity for transformation through innovation and technology.

The advent of Artificial Intelligence (AI) and Machine Learning (ML) has sparked a global revolution in how industries operate, governments function, and societies advance. These technologies are capable of solving problems at a scale and speed previously unimaginable. Nigeria, like many other developing nations, stands at a crossroads: it can either embrace these technological advancements and harness their potential to solve its most pressing problems, or it can lag behind, missing an opportunity to leapfrog traditional development challenges. This book is born out of the belief that Nigeria can leverage AI and ML to address its unique challenges and accelerate its development.

In this book, I explore the application of AI and ML in addressing some of Nigeria's most critical issues. Through a detailed examination of various sectors agriculture, healthcare, education, governance, security, energy, transportation, and more, this book aims to provide a roadmap for how AI can be effectively used to not only alleviate these problems but also to propel Nigeria towards becoming a leader in technological innovation on the African continent and beyond.

The objective is not merely to highlight the potential of AI but to ground the discussion in Nigeria's specific context, recognizing that successful implementation requires more than just technology. It necessitates an ecosystem that includes appropriate policies, human capital development, ethical considerations, and a vision for long-term sustainability. Nigeria's challenges may be daunting, but with the right approach, they are not insurmountable. AI offers tools that can make a profound difference.

It is my hope that this book will inspire policymakers, business leaders, technologists, academics, and citizens alike to embrace the possibilities that AI and ML offer. It is also intended to provoke meaningful dialogue about the future of technology in Nigeria and to offer practical insights into how these tools can be applied to create a better, more prosperous, and equitable society for all.

INTRODUCTION

Nigeria is a country of extraordinary promise. With over 200 million people, it is the most populous country in Africa and has the largest economy on the continent. Its rich natural resources, youthful population, and strategic geographic position make it a key player in both regional and global affairs. Yet, Nigeria is also a country facing significant challenges. High levels of poverty, unemployment, infrastructural deficiencies, and political instability have held back its progress. In many respects, Nigeria's growth has been stunted by its inability to overcome these structural problems.

In recent years, however, technology has emerged as a possible solution to many of the challenges facing Nigeria. While traditional approaches to development have often fallen short, the rise of digital technologies, particularly Artificial Intelligence (AI) and Machine Learning (ML) has opened up new possibilities for addressing these issues in innovative ways. AI and ML are reshaping industries and societies across the world, and Nigeria has the opportunity to harness these technologies to create solutions that are specifically tailored to its unique challenges.

AI is essentially the simulation of human intelligence by machines. It involves the use of algorithms and computational power to process vast amounts of data and make decisions based on that data.

Machine Learning, a subset of AI, is focused on enabling machines to learn from data, improve their performance over time, and make increasingly accurate predictions or decisions. These technologies are already transforming industries globally, from healthcare to agriculture, from education to finance, and from energy to transportation. They offer immense potential for developing countries like Nigeria, where the need for innovation is particularly urgent.

The importance of applying AI to Nigeria's context cannot be overstated. For a country that has struggled with inefficiencies in almost every sector, AI offers the promise of greater precision, better decision-making, and more efficient use of resources. In agriculture, for instance, AI can help optimize crop yields, monitor soil conditions, and predict weather patterns, which could help address the country's food security issues. In healthcare, AI can assist in diagnosing diseases, managing patient records, and even predicting outbreaks of illnesses, which is crucial in a country where access to quality healthcare is often limited. In education, AI-powered tools can help bridge the gap in learning outcomes, providing personalized educational experiences to students regardless of their geographical location.

Governance is another area where AI can make a significant impact. Nigeria has long struggled with inefficiencies in public service delivery, corruption, and a lack of transparency. AI can help automate many aspects of government processes, reducing opportunities for corruption, improving service delivery, and increasing transparency and accountability. Moreover, AI can be used to predict and prevent security threats, whether they come in the form of insurgency, terrorism, or cybercrime, all of which are significant concerns in Nigeria.

However, the potential of AI and ML in Nigeria extends beyond addressing specific sectoral challenges. These technologies can also help drive economic growth by fostering innovation and creating new industries. Nigeria's tech sector, often referred to as "Silicon Lagos," has already begun to make strides in this direction, with a growing number of startups focusing on AI-driven solutions for problems ranging from financial inclusion to logistics. The growth of this sector could create millions of jobs, especially for Nigeria's youthful population, and position the country as a technological leader in Africa.

Yet, despite the potential benefits, the widespread adoption of AI and ML in Nigeria is not without its challenges. The country faces significant barriers to the implementation of these technologies, including a lack of infrastructure, limited access to high-quality data, and a shortage of skilled professionals. In addition, there are ethical concerns related to the use of AI, such as privacy, data security, and the risk of exacerbating existing inequalities. Policymakers must be proactive in addressing these issues to ensure that the benefits of AI are equitably distributed across society.

Furthermore, the successful application of AI and ML in Nigeria will require a coordinated effort between the government, private sector, academia, and civil society. Governments must create enabling environments through policies and regulations that support innovation while also safeguarding against the potential risks. The private sector must invest in developing AI-driven solutions that address local needs. Academia must play a key role in training the next generation of AI professionals and conducting research that advances the field. Civil society, on the other hand, must engage in discussions about the ethical use of AI and advocate for its responsible application.

This book aims to explore the many ways in which AI and ML can be applied to solve Nigeria's unique challenges. Each chapter will delve into a specific sector or issue, examining how AI can be used to create innovative solutions, improve efficiency, and ultimately contribute to the country's development. From agriculture to healthcare, from education to energy, and from governance to security, AI offers a new set of tools for tackling Nigeria's most pressing problems.

As we move forward into an increasingly digital world, Nigeria must not be left behind. The country has the opportunity to harness AI and ML to transform its future, but doing so will require vision, investment, and collaboration. It will also require a commitment to ensuring that these technologies are used in ways that benefit all Nigerians, not just a select few. By embracing AI and ML, Nigeria can address its challenges in ways that are innovative, efficient, and sustainable, paving the way for a brighter future.

This is a pivotal moment in Nigeria's history. The choices made today regarding AI and technology will shape the country's future for generations to come. This book seeks to provide a roadmap for how Nigeria can seize this moment, leveraging AI and ML to solve its unique challenges and unlock its full potential.

CHAPTER 1
Understanding AI and Machine Learning

A rtificial Intelligence (AI) and Machine Learning (ML) are often regarded as the most transformative technological advances of the 21st century, reshaping industries, businesses, governments, and even daily life in profound ways. While these terms may conjure images of robots or futuristic technology, AI and ML are already deeply embedded in systems and tools we use every day, from smartphone applications to complex systems that power the global economy. To fully appreciate the potential of AI and ML in addressing Nigeria's unique challenges, it is essential to understand what these technologies are, how they function, and their potential impact on diverse sectors.

At its core, Artificial Intelligence refers to the ability of machines to perform tasks that typically require human intelligence, such as problem-solving, decision-making, visual perception, language comprehension, and even creative endeavors. These systems are designed to process massive amounts of data, identify patterns, and make informed decisions based on the information they process. What differentiates AI from traditional computer systems is its capability to learn and improve over time by analyzing data and adjusting its approach to produce more accurate results.

Machine Learning, a subset of AI, specifically focuses on enabling machines to learn from data without being explicitly programmed for every task. Historically, computers could only perform specific tasks when coded to do so, but Machine Learning has changed that paradigm by allowing computers to learn from examples. A machine learning model is trained in data and, through this training, learns to make predictions or identify patterns. For instance, an ML algorithm trained on thousands of medical records can learn to identify patterns that indicate the presence of a disease, even if it has never encountered a particular case before. This ability to generalize from past data allows the model to adapt and improve its accuracy with more data over time.

The reason AI and ML are so powerful lies in their ability to process and analyze vast datasets at speeds and scales that human capabilities could never match. In today's data-driven world, information is being generated at an unprecedented rate. From social media interactions to financial transactions, from sensor data in cities to health data from wearable devices, the amount of information produced is staggering. AI thrives on this abundance of data, using sophisticated algorithms to detect meaningful patterns that help in decision-making. The volume and variety of data available today mean that AI can be applied to an ever-growing number of fields.

On a global scale, AI has already begun transforming industries. In healthcare, AI-powered diagnostic tools are now able to analyze medical images with a level of accuracy that rivals or even surpasses that of human specialists. In agriculture, AI models predict crop yields, monitoring soil health, and optimizing the use of resources like fertilizers and water. The finance sector has embraced AI for detecting fraudulent transactions, improving credit scoring methods, and automating customer service with chatbots. AI's potential applications are vast and varied, and the rate at which this technology is advancing continues to accelerate, opening up new possibilities across sectors.

For Nigeria, the application of AI and ML holds exceptional promise. The country faces a wide range of unique challenges, many of which have proven resistant to conventional methods of problem-solving. From healthcare inefficiencies and agricultural productivity gaps to educational disparities and governance bottlenecks, these problems often arise from systemic inefficiencies, inadequate infrastructure, and a lack of access to actionable data. AI offers a new pathway to address many of these issues by enabling better decision-making, improving the allocation of resources, and providing insights that can spark innovation.

In agriculture, for instance, Nigeria's economy depends heavily on farming, yet the sector continues to grapple with outdated practices and poor yields. AI could revolutionize agricultural practices through predictive models that advise farmers on the optimal times to plant, fertilize, or harvest crops. These models can predict weather patterns, anticipate pest outbreaks, and offer suggestions to maximize yields while minimizing environmental impacts. Similarly, in healthcare, AI can enhance diagnosis and patient care by assisting doctors in rural areas, where specialists are scarce, by providing diagnostic tools that can analyze symptoms and medical images with high accuracy.

However, the widespread adoption of AI in Nigeria faces significant hurdles. One of the major barriers is the lack of infrastructure to support the extensive use of AI technologies. High-speed internet connectivity, stable electricity, and access to large, quality datasets are all prerequisites for the successful deployment of AI solutions. Nigeria continues to experience power supply inconsistencies and limited broadband penetration, which hampers the scalability of AI-driven solutions. For AI to flourish, these infrastructural issues must be addressed as a priority.

Another challenge is access to data. AI's strength lies in its ability to process and learn from large datasets, but many sectors in Nigeria still lack the systems and frameworks to collect, store, and analyze data in structured and usable formats. Data is often fragmented, unavailable, or unreliable, making it difficult to implement AI solutions that depend on the constant influx of accurate information.

Moreover, there is a shortage of skilled professionals trained in AI and data science. While Nigeria has a burgeoning tech scene, much of the talent has been concentrated in the fintech space, and relatively few experts work on AI-related projects in sectors like agriculture, healthcare, or governance. This skills gap poses a serious barrier to the broader adoption of AI technologies. To fully leverage AI, Nigeria will need to invest in building a robust talent pool through targeted education, training programs, and initiatives to attract more individuals into the field of AI research and development.

Despite these challenges, the potential benefits of AI for Nigeria are immense. With the right investments, strategic planning, and a focus on overcoming infrastructural and skills gaps, AI could dramatically reshape key sectors and solve some of the country's most intractable problems. AI's ability to process vast amounts of information quickly and accurately could lead to insights that revolutionize the way Nigeria addresses its challenges in healthcare, education, agriculture, and beyond.

It is also essential to acknowledge that technology alone is not a panacea. AI can significantly enhance decision-making, automate processes, and provide efficiencies, but it must be integrated into existing systems and deployed in a way that complements human expertise. Furthermore, the ethical implications of AI, particularly in terms of data privacy, bias, and inequality, must be considered carefully. AI systems, if not properly managed, can exacerbate existing social inequalities or introduce new forms of discrimination. The collection and use of data must be transparent, and AI systems should be designed with fairness and accountability in mind to ensure that the benefits of AI are equitably distributed across society.

In conclusion, Artificial Intelligence and Machine Learning offer Nigeria a powerful toolkit for addressing its unique challenges across a wide range of sectors. The ability to analyze data on a scale, learn from patterns, and make informed decisions has the potential to revolutionize industries and improve quality of life. However, achieving this potential will require Nigeria to invest in the necessary infrastructure, build its talent pool, and develop policies that promote innovation while safeguarding ethical concerns. The future of AI in Nigeria is promising, but it will depend on how well the country can navigate the challenges and opportunities that this transformative technology brings.

CHAPTER 2
Nigeria's Unique Challenges an Overview

Nigeria, often hailed as a country of immense potential, is simultaneously beset by deep-rooted and complex challenges. As Africa's most populous nation and its largest economy, Nigeria boasts a wealth of natural resources, a burgeoning youthful population, and an entrepreneurial spirit that positions it as a potential powerhouse both on the continent and globally. However, the country continues to struggle with numerous interrelated issues that have slowed its development and exacerbated socio-economic inequalities. Understanding these challenges is vital when exploring how Artificial Intelligence (AI) and Machine Learning (ML) can be harnessed to address Nigeria's pressing problems and help unlock its full potential.

One of Nigeria's most significant challenges is widespread poverty. Despite its vast natural resources, particularly oil, which accounts for a significant portion of the country's GDP and government revenues, much of Nigeria's population remains impoverished. Approximately 40% of the population lives below the poverty line, according to World Bank estimates. This economic inequality is further exacerbated by high levels of unemployment and underemployment, particularly among the youth. Nigeria's economy, while large, remains overly reliant on oil exports, leaving it vulnerable to fluctuations in global oil prices. Diversifying the economy, with a focus on sectors like agriculture, manufacturing, and technology, is critical for long-term sustainability, but progress in this area has been slow.

The issue of poverty is closely linked to another fundamental problem: inequality. Economic growth in Nigeria has not been inclusive, leading to a widening gap between the rich and the poor. Income disparities are stark, and access to essential services such as healthcare, education, and clean water is unevenly distributed across the country, with rural areas particularly disadvantaged. This inequality is not only economic but also geographical, as the northern region of Nigeria has lagged behind in terms of development compared to the more prosperous southern states. Addressing these disparities is crucial for national stability and development, as marginalized populations are more likely to experience social unrest and insurgency.

Infrastructure is another critical challenge facing Nigeria. The country's infrastructure, from electricity to transportation to water supply, is inadequate for a rapidly growing population and an expanding economy. Chronic power shortages are perhaps the most glaring example, with Nigeria's electricity supply being notoriously unreliable. Businesses and households alike depend heavily on costly and polluting diesel generators to supplement the unreliable national grid. The World Bank estimates that Nigeria loses approximately $29 billion annually due to its inadequate power supply. Without a stable and reliable energy infrastructure, economic growth is stifled, productivity is reduced, and foreign investment is discouraged.

In addition to power shortages, Nigeria's transportation infrastructure is underdeveloped. Roads, railways, and public transportation systems are often inadequate to meet the needs of the population, particularly in urban areas like Lagos, where traffic congestion is a constant problem. Poor infrastructure hampers not only economic activity but also access to essential services, particularly in rural areas where poor roads and inadequate public transportation limit access to healthcare, education, and markets. Healthcare is another sector that faces significant challenges. Nigeria's healthcare system is underfunded, understaffed, and often inaccessible to large segments of the population. Rural areas, in particular, face severe shortages of medical professionals and healthcare facilities. As a result, healthcare outcomes in Nigeria remain poor, with high maternal and infant mortality rates and a high prevalence of communicable diseases such as malaria and tuberculosis. The COVID-19 pandemic exposed and exacerbated the vulnerabilities in Nigeria's healthcare system, highlighting the urgent need for investment, innovation, and reform in this critical sector. The integration of AI and ML into healthcare could play a transformative role in improving healthcare delivery, particularly by expanding access to diagnostic tools and medical expertise in underserved areas.

Education, too, remains a significant challenge in Nigeria. Although the country has made progress in improving access to education, particularly at the primary level, millions of children remain out of school, particularly in the northern regions where insecurity and poverty are more prevalent. Even when students do have access to education, the quality of that education is often lacking. Many schools suffer from overcrowded classrooms, a shortage of qualified teachers, and inadequate learning materials. The digital divide further exacerbates educational inequalities, as many students in rural areas do not have access to the technology and internet connectivity necessary for modern learning. Bridging this digital divide is essential if Nigeria is to develop a workforce capable of competing in the global knowledge economy.

In addition to these socio-economic challenges, Nigeria also faces critical governance issues. Weak institutions, inefficiency, and corruption have long plagued Nigeria's government at multiple levels. These issues have eroded public trust in government institutions and hindered progress in areas such as infrastructure development, economic reform, and public service delivery. Corruption has been particularly problematic in the allocation and management of public resources, with funds often siphoned off before they can be used for their intended purposes. Strengthening governance, reducing corruption, and improving the efficiency and transparency of public institutions are essential if Nigeria is to achieve sustainable development.

Security concerns represent another major challenge for Nigeria. The country has been plagued by insurgency, terrorism, and violent conflict, particularly in the northern region, where the Islamist militant group Boko Haram has been active for more than a decade. Boko Haram's insurgency has resulted in the displacement of millions of people, as well as widespread violence and destruction. In addition to the threat posed by Boko Haram, Nigeria has also experienced violence in the Niger Delta region, where conflicts over resource control, environmental degradation, and political marginalization have fueled unrest. In urban areas, crime, including kidnapping, armed robbery, and cybercrime, has also been on the rise, further contributing to a climate of insecurity that discourages investment and economic growth.

Environmental challenges are another critical concern for Nigeria, particularly as the effects of climate change become more pronounced. The country is vulnerable to a range of environmental risks, including desertification in the north, rising sea levels in coastal areas, and increased flooding during the rainy season. Deforestation, pollution, and the over-exploitation of natural resources have further exacerbated environmental degradation. Addressing these issues is essential for ensuring a sustainable future for Nigeria's growing population, as environmental damage not only threatens livelihoods but also increases the risk of conflict and social unrest.

Despite these challenges, Nigeria is a nation of resilience and innovation. The country has a dynamic and entrepreneurial population, particularly among its youth, who are eager to embrace new technologies and develop solutions to the problems they face. The rise of Nigeria's tech sector, particularly in cities like Lagos, has demonstrated the potential for technology to drive economic growth and social change. Nigeria's "Silicon Lagos" is home to a growing number of tech startups that are leveraging digital tools to create innovative solutions in areas such as financial services, agriculture, and education.

Artificial Intelligence and Machine Learning represent the next frontier in this technological revolution. By leveraging these technologies, Nigeria has the opportunity to develop solutions that are tailored to its specific needs and challenges. AI can be used to improve agricultural productivity, optimize healthcare delivery, enhance education, and strengthen governance. It can also play a key role in addressing security issues, enabling more effective surveillance, intelligence gathering, and crime prevention efforts.

However, for AI to be successfully applied to Nigeria's challenges, a number of conditions must be met. First and foremost, there must be investment in the necessary infrastructure, including reliable electricity and high-speed internet, which are critical for the deployment of AI-powered solutions. Second, there must be access to high-quality data, as AI systems rely on large datasets to function effectively. Third, Nigeria must develop the human capital needed to support the growth of its AI industry, which will require significant investment in education and training programs. Finally, there must be a regulatory framework that supports innovation while addressing the ethical and social implications of AI, such as data privacy, security, and the risk of bias.

In conclusion, the challenges Nigeria faces are complex and multifaceted, but they are not insurmountable. By embracing Artificial Intelligence and Machine Learning, Nigeria has the opportunity to develop innovative solutions that are not only effective but also sustainable and scalable. With the right investments, partnerships, and strategic planning, Nigeria can leverage AI to address its most pressing challenges, unlock its economic potential, and create a more prosperous, equitable, and resilient society for all its citizens.

CHAPTER 3
AI in Agriculture Enhancing Food Security

Agriculture has long been one of the most important sectors in Nigeria's economy, providing livelihoods for a significant portion of the population and contributing to the country's GDP. Despite this importance, the sector has struggled with inefficiencies, low productivity, and vulnerability to external shocks such as climate change and pest infestations. These challenges have led to a reliance on food imports to meet the country's growing demand, raising concerns about food security. Artificial Intelligence (AI) and Machine Learning (ML) offer transformative potential in the agricultural sector by providing tools that can increase productivity, reduce waste, optimize resource use, and make farming more resilient to environmental changes.

One of the primary challenges facing Nigerian agriculture is the lack of access to reliable data. Many farmers, particularly smallholder farmers, make decisions based on intuition or limited information, often leading to suboptimal outcomes. For example, farmers may not have access to accurate weather forecasts, soil condition data, or market prices, which can lead to poor planting and harvesting decisions, inefficient use of water and fertilizers, and an inability to respond to changing market conditions. AI can help fill this information gap by providing farmers with real-time data and predictive analytics that enable them to make more informed decisions.

AI-powered platforms can analyze data on weather patterns, soil health, crop conditions, and market trends, providing farmers with actionable insights that help them optimize their farming practices. For instance, AI algorithms can analyze historical weather data and current atmospheric conditions to predict future weather patterns with greater accuracy. This allows farmers to anticipate droughts, floods, or other adverse weather conditions, helping them make timely decisions about planting, irrigation, and harvesting. Additionally, AI can monitor soil health by analyzing data from sensors placed in fields, providing recommendations on the optimal use of fertilizers and water to maximize crop yields while minimizing environmental impact.

Precision farming is one area where AI can have a particularly profound impact. Precision farming involves using AI, sensors, drones, and other technologies to monitor crops and manage agricultural practices more efficiently. Drones equipped with AI-powered cameras and sensors can scan fields to detect early signs of pest infestations, nutrient deficiencies, or diseases. By identifying problems before they become severe, farmers can take targeted actions, such as applying pesticides or adjusting irrigation practices, to protect their crops. This reduces the need for blanket pesticide applications, lowers costs, and minimizes environmental damage.

Another area where AI can drive improvements in agriculture is in water management. Water is a scarce resource in many parts of Nigeria, and inefficient irrigation practices can lead to significant water waste. AI-powered smart irrigation systems can monitor soil moisture levels in real-time and automatically adjust irrigation schedules to ensure that crops receive the right amount of water when they need it. By optimizing water use, these systems help conserve water resources while maintaining or even increasing crop yields. In regions where water scarcity is a critical issue, such as northern Nigeria, these technologies could make a substantial difference in agricultural sustainability and food security.

AI can also play a critical role in addressing one of the most persistent challenges in Nigerian agriculture: the inefficiency of supply chains. Many farmers struggle to get their products to market due to poor infrastructure, lack of access to reliable transportation, and limited information about market demand. Perishable goods, such as fruits and vegetables, often spoil before reaching consumers, leading to high levels of food waste. AI-driven supply chain management platforms can help optimize logistics by predicting demand, monitoring transportation routes, and connecting farmers directly with buyers. By improving the efficiency of the supply chain, AI can reduce food waste, increase farmers' incomes, and ensure that consumers have access to fresh, affordable produce.

In addition to crop production, AI has the potential to revolutionize livestock farming in Nigeria. AI-powered tools can be used to monitor the health of livestock, detect diseases early, and optimize feeding practices. For example, sensors and cameras can be placed in barns or pastures to track the behavior and movement of animals, detecting signs of illness or distress. AI algorithms can then analyze this data to recommend interventions, such as changes in diet or medical treatment, to improve the health and productivity of livestock. Early detection of diseases can help prevent the spread of infections, reducing mortality rates and improving overall farm profitability.

Agricultural financing is another area where AI can make a significant impact. Many smallholder farmers in Nigeria struggle to access credit because they lack formal financial histories or collateral. This limits their ability to invest in modern farming technologies or expand their operations. AI can help bridge this gap by analyzing alternative data sources, such as mobile phone usage, farming practices, and weather patterns, to assess the creditworthiness of farmers. By providing more accurate and comprehensive risk assessments, AI can enable financial institutions to offer loans to farmers who would otherwise be excluded from the formal financial system. This can increase investment in agriculture, helping farmers adopt new technologies and improve their productivity.

However, despite the potential of AI to transform agriculture in Nigeria, there are several barriers to its widespread adoption. One of the main challenges is the digital divide, particularly in rural areas where many farmers lack access to smartphones, the internet, or the digital literacy needed to use AI-powered tools effectively. Even when these technologies are available, there is often a lack of awareness among farmers about how to integrate them into their farming practices. To address this challenge, there will need to be significant investment in digital infrastructure, training programs, and awareness campaigns to ensure that farmers can fully benefit from AI technologies.

Another challenge is the cost of implementing AI solutions. While large commercial farms may be able to afford the necessary infrastructure and technologies, smallholder farmers who make up the majority of Nigeria's agricultural sector may find it difficult to make such investments. To address this issue, partnerships between the government, private sector, and development organizations will be essential to making AI technologies more affordable and accessible to small-scale farmers. This could include providing subsidies, offering low-interest loans, or creating cooperatives where farmers can pool their resources to invest in AI-powered tools.

There are also ethical and legal considerations related to the use of AI in agriculture. For example, the collection and use of data from farms raise questions about data ownership and privacy. Farmers may be concerned about how their data is being used, who has access to it, and whether they are receiving a fair share of the benefits generated from the use of that data. These issues will need to be addressed through clear regulations and guidelines to protect farmers' rights and ensure that the benefits of AI are shared equitably.

Despite these challenges, the potential benefits of AI in agriculture are immense. By improving productivity, reducing waste, optimizing resource use, and making farming more resilient to climate change, AI can play a critical role in enhancing food security in Nigeria. The integration of AI into agriculture can also create new opportunities for economic growth, as Nigeria moves towards a more modern and efficient agricultural sector. Given that agriculture is the primary source of livelihood for millions of Nigerians, these innovations could have a transformative impact on both the economy and the well-being of the population.

As Nigeria continues to face challenges related to population growth, urbanization, and climate change, the need for sustainable and efficient agricultural practices will become even more urgent. AI offers a powerful set of tools that can help address these challenges, but its success will depend on how well these technologies are integrated into existing farming systems and made accessible to farmers, regardless of their location or financial status. By investing in AI and building the necessary infrastructure, Nigeria can position itself as a leader in agricultural innovation, ensuring a more secure and prosperous future for its people.

CHAPTER 4
Improving Healthcare Delivery with AI

Nigeria's healthcare system faces numerous challenges that affect the quality and accessibility of medical services, particularly for those living in rural and underserved areas. These challenges include inadequate infrastructure, a shortage of healthcare professionals, inefficient resource allocation, and limited access to diagnostic tools and treatments. For millions of Nigerians, especially those in isolated regions, healthcare remains a luxury rather than a right, contributing to poor health outcomes, high mortality rates, and the persistent spread of communicable diseases. The COVID-19 pandemic has further exposed the fragility of Nigeria's healthcare system, highlighting the urgent need for innovation and investment in healthcare delivery.

Artificial Intelligence (AI) offers a promising solution to many of these healthcare challenges by enhancing the efficiency, accessibility, and quality of medical services. By leveraging AI technologies, Nigeria can transform its healthcare system, enabling it to deliver more effective and affordable healthcare, particularly in underserved communities. AI's ability to process vast amounts of data, analyze complex medical patterns, and provide predictive insights can revolutionize healthcare delivery in Nigeria, making it more responsive to the needs of the population.

One of the most significant ways in which AI can improve healthcare delivery in Nigeria is through early diagnosis and disease detection. In many parts of the country, access to diagnostic tools is limited, resulting in delayed diagnoses and treatments, particularly for diseases that require specialized knowledge, such as cancer, tuberculosis, or diabetes. AI-powered diagnostic tools can help bridge this gap by analyzing medical data, such as images or patient records, to detect diseases early and with high accuracy. For instance, AI algorithms can analyze X-rays, CT scans, or MRI images to detect conditions such as pneumonia, fractures, or tumors. These systems can often identify abnormalities that may be missed by human doctors, particularly in rural areas where there may be a shortage of specialists.

AI diagnostic systems also have the advantage of being scalable and deployable in remote areas. For example, mobile health clinics equipped with AI diagnostic tools could travel to rural communities, providing medical services to populations that would otherwise lack access to basic healthcare. AI systems could analyze patient data on-site, enabling healthcare workers to make more accurate diagnoses and recommend appropriate treatments without the need to transport patients to distant hospitals. This would not only improve health outcomes but also reduce the costs associated with patient transfers and hospital admissions.

Another major area where AI can have a transformative impact is in predictive analytics, which involves using data to predict future health outcomes and identify high-risk patients before they develop serious conditions. For example, AI algorithms can analyze data from electronic health records (EHRs), wearable devices, and other health data sources to identify patients who are at risk of developing chronic conditions such as hypertension, diabetes, or heart disease. By identifying these high-risk individuals early, healthcare providers can implement preventive measures, such as lifestyle interventions or medication, to reduce the likelihood of the condition progressing. Predictive analytics can also help healthcare providers allocate resources more effectively by prioritizing patients based on their risk profiles and ensuring that those who need care the most receive timely interventions.

In addition to early diagnosis and predictive analytics, AI can significantly improve access to healthcare through telemedicine and remote consultations. Nigeria has a large and geographically dispersed population, with many rural communities located far from healthcare facilities. AI-powered telemedicine platforms can connect patients in remote areas with healthcare providers in urban centers, enabling them to receive medical consultations, diagnoses, and treatment recommendations without having to travel long distances. These platforms can use AI to triage patients, assess the severity of their conditions, and prioritize cases based on urgency. AI-driven chatbots can also provide basic health advice, answer common medical questions, and assist patients in navigating the healthcare system, reducing the burden on overworked healthcare professionals.

AI can also play a key role in optimizing the allocation of healthcare resources, which is a major challenge in Nigeria's healthcare system. Hospitals and clinics often face shortages of critical resources, including hospital beds, medical equipment, and medications. AI algorithms can analyze data on patient admissions, disease outbreaks, and resource availability to predict demand for healthcare services and optimize the allocation of resources. For instance, during an infectious disease outbreak, AI can help predict where the highest demand for hospital beds, ventilators, or medications will be, ensuring that resources are distributed accordingly. This can improve the overall efficiency of the healthcare system, reduce waiting times, and ensure that resources are available where they are needed most.

One of the most pressing challenges in Nigeria's healthcare system is the shortage of skilled healthcare professionals, including doctors, nurses, and specialists. The doctor-to-patient ratio in Nigeria is far below the recommended levels set by the World Health Organization (WHO), and this shortage is particularly acute in rural areas. AI can help alleviate some of this burden by automating routine tasks, such as patient record-keeping, appointment scheduling, and medication management. By reducing the administrative workload on healthcare workers, AI allows doctors and nurses to focus more on patient care, improving the overall quality of healthcare services.

AI can also assist healthcare professionals in decision-making by providing evidence-based recommendations for diagnosis and treatment. For instance, AI algorithms can analyze vast amounts of medical literature, clinical guidelines, and patient data to suggest the most effective treatment options for a given patient. This can be particularly valuable in rural areas where healthcare workers may lack access to the latest medical research or may not have the expertise to manage complex cases. AI-powered decision-making support systems can provide healthcare workers with real-time insights, enabling them to make more informed decisions and improve patient outcomes.

In addition to improving healthcare delivery, AI can play a crucial role in public health by helping to predict and manage disease outbreaks. AI algorithms can analyze data from various sources, such as social media, news reports, satellite imagery, and healthcare records, to detect patterns that indicate the emergence of a disease outbreak. For example, AI can analyze patterns of hospital admissions, reports of symptoms on social media, or environmental factors such as changes in temperature or humidity to predict the spread of infectious diseases such as malaria, cholera, or Ebola. By identifying these patterns early, public health officials can implement measures to contain the outbreak before it spreads widely. AI can also be used to model the potential spread of infectious diseases and predict the impact of different interventions, such as vaccination campaigns or quarantine measures. This type of predictive modeling can be invaluable in managing public health crises and reducing the spread of diseases.

However, while AI has the potential to revolutionize healthcare delivery in Nigeria, there are significant challenges that must be addressed to ensure its successful implementation. One of the main challenges is the lack of digital infrastructure, particularly in rural areas where access to reliable electricity and internet connectivity is limited. AI-powered healthcare solutions often rely on internet connectivity, cloud computing, and access to digital medical records, but many healthcare facilities in Nigeria still rely on paper-based systems. To fully benefit from AI technologies, there will need to be significant investment in upgrading the digital infrastructure of the healthcare system, ensuring that all healthcare facilities have access to the necessary tools to implement AI solutions.

Another critical challenge is the issue of data privacy and security. Healthcare data is highly sensitive, and the use of AI raises concerns about how patient data is collected, stored, and used. There must be clear regulations and guidelines in place to protect patient privacy and ensure that healthcare data is used ethically. Additionally, AI algorithms are only as good as the data they are trained on, and there is a risk that AI systems could perpetuate biases if they are trained on incomplete or biased data. For example, if an AI system is trained on data that does not reflect the diversity of Nigeria's population, it may make inaccurate predictions or recommendations for certain groups of people. Ensuring that AI systems are trained on diverse and representative datasets will be essential to avoid these issues and ensure that AI benefits all patients.

In conclusion, AI has the potential to transform healthcare delivery in Nigeria by improving diagnosis, increasing access to healthcare, optimizing resource allocation, and assisting healthcare professionals in decision-making. By embracing AI, Nigeria can improve the efficiency and quality of its healthcare system, ensuring that more people have access to the care they need, particularly in underserved areas. However, to fully realize the benefits of AI in healthcare, there will need to be investments in digital infrastructure, training for healthcare workers, and regulatory frameworks to address privacy and ethical concerns. With the right approach, AI can play a pivotal role in improving health outcomes and reducing healthcare inequalities in Nigeria, creating a more resilient and responsive healthcare system for all.

CHAPTER 5
Education and AI Bridging the Learning Gap

Education is one of the most critical determinants of a country's future prosperity. In Nigeria, however, the education sector faces numerous challenges that hinder the ability of millions of children and young adults to access quality education. Despite progress in expanding access to education, there are still millions of children out of school, particularly in rural and conflict-affected regions. For those who are in school, the quality of education is often lacking, with overcrowded classrooms, poorly trained teachers, and insufficient learning materials. Furthermore, the digital divide exacerbates educational inequality, as many students in rural areas do not have access to the technology and internet connectivity necessary for modern learning. These challenges are particularly acute in a country with a rapidly growing population, where the demand for education is outpacing the government's ability to provide it.

Artificial Intelligence (AI) offers the potential to transform education in Nigeria by bridging the learning gap, personalizing education, enhancing teacher effectiveness, and providing students with access to high-quality educational resources, regardless of their location. By leveraging AI technologies, Nigeria can create an education system that is more inclusive, equitable, and responsive to the needs of its diverse student population.

One of the most significant ways AI can improve education in Nigeria is through personalized learning. Traditional education systems often follow a one-size-fits-all approach, where all students are taught the same material at the same pace, regardless of their individual learning needs. However, students have different strengths, weaknesses, and learning styles, and some may struggle to keep up with the curriculum, while others may not be sufficiently challenged. AI-powered educational platforms can help address this issue by adapting to the needs of individual students and providing personalized learning experiences.

AI systems can analyze data on students' learning patterns, such as their performance on quizzes, homework, and tests, to identify areas where they are struggling or excelling. Based on this analysis, the AI platform can recommend personalized learning materials, such as videos, exercises, or reading assignments, that are tailored to the student's needs. For example, if a student is struggling with a particular math concept, the AI system can provide additional resources, such as interactive tutorials or practice problems, to help the student improve in that area. Similarly, if a student is excelling in a subject, the AI system can recommend more challenging material to keep the student engaged and motivated. This personalized approach can help ensure that students receive the support they need to succeed, regardless of their starting point.

In addition to personalized learning, AI can enhance the effectiveness of teachers by providing them with tools to monitor student performance and identify areas where intervention is needed. Teachers often struggle to track the progress of large numbers of students, particularly in overcrowded classrooms where individual attention is limited. AI-powered platforms can analyze student data to identify patterns of underperformance or disengagement, allowing teachers to provide targeted support to students who may be falling behind. For example, an AI system could alert a teacher if a student's performance has declined over a period of time, prompting the teacher to intervene and provide additional help.

AI can also assist teachers in creating more engaging and interactive learning experiences. AI-driven virtual tutors or educational chatbots can provide students with instant feedback on their work, answer their questions, and guide them through complex topics. These tools can supplement traditional teaching methods and provide students with additional support outside of the classroom. For instance, if a student is struggling with a homework assignment, they can ask an AI tutor for help and receive immediate feedback, rather than waiting for the next class to ask the teacher. This can improve student engagement and help them stay on track with their learning.

Access to quality educational resources is another area where AI can make a significant impact, particularly in rural and underserved areas where students may not have access to the same educational materials as their urban counterparts. AI-powered platforms can provide students with access to high-quality digital content, such as textbooks, videos, and interactive lessons, which can be accessed from smartphones, tablets, or computers. These platforms can be used to supplement traditional classroom learning or provide educational opportunities for students who are unable to attend school due to geographic or financial barriers.

For example, in remote areas where there are no schools or qualified teachers, AI-powered educational platforms could be used to deliver lessons and learning materials directly to students through mobile devices. Students could access a wide range of subjects, from math and science to language arts and social studies, and the platform could provide personalized learning paths based on the student's interests and needs. AI can also help bridge language barriers by providing real-time translation services, enabling students who speak different languages to access educational materials in their native language. This could be particularly valuable in a country like Nigeria, where there are hundreds of different languages spoken across the country.

In addition to improving access to educational resources, AI can play a key role in assessing student performance. Traditional assessments, such as standardized tests, often fail to capture the full range of a student's abilities and may not provide a complete picture of their strengths and weaknesses. AI-powered assessment tools can provide more comprehensive and dynamic evaluations of student performance, going beyond test scores to assess factors such as critical thinking, creativity, and problem-solving skills. These tools can analyze data from a variety of sources, including quizzes, assignments, and classroom participation, to provide a more holistic assessment of a student's abilities. This can help educators develop more effective teaching strategies and tailor their instruction to meet the needs of individual students.

AI also has the potential to transform vocational education and skills development, which are critical for addressing Nigeria's youth unemployment crisis. Many young people in Nigeria lack the skills needed to compete in the modern job market, particularly in industries that require technical expertise. AI-powered platforms can provide learners with access to online courses and training programs that teach practical skills in fields such as coding, data analysis, digital marketing, and entrepreneurship. These platforms can use AI to recommend courses based on a learner's interests, career goals, and skill level, ensuring that they acquire the skills most relevant to their future careers. Moreover, AI can provide real-time feedback on practical exercises, helping learners develop hands-on skills that are essential in the workforce.

However, while AI offers significant opportunities to improve education in Nigeria, there are also challenges that must be addressed. One of the main challenges is the digital divide, particularly in rural areas where access to the internet and digital devices is limited. To fully benefit from AI-powered educational tools, students need access to reliable internet connectivity and the necessary devices to use these platforms. Without this infrastructure, students in rural and underserved areas may continue to be left behind, exacerbating educational inequality.

Addressing this issue will require investment in digital infrastructure, particularly in rural and remote regions. This could involve expanding access to high-speed internet, providing affordable mobile devices for students, and developing offline versions of AI-powered educational platforms that can be used in areas with limited connectivity. Governments, private sector companies, and international development organizations will need to collaborate to ensure that digital education is accessible to all students, regardless of their location or socio-economic status.

Another challenge is the need for teaching training. While AI can provide valuable tools to enhance teaching, teachers must be trained to use these tools effectively. This will require investment in professional development programs that equip teachers with the skills to integrate AI into their teaching practices. Teachers will need to understand how to use AI-powered platforms to monitor student progress, personalize learning, and provide targeted support to students. Additionally, teachers will need to be trained in the ethical and privacy considerations related to the use of AI in education, ensuring that student data is used responsibly and transparently.

Data privacy is another important consideration. AI-powered educational platforms rely on large amounts of data to function effectively, but there are concerns about how this data is collected, stored, and used. Student data is highly sensitive, and it is essential that clear regulations and guidelines are in place to protect student privacy and ensure that data is used ethically. Schools and education providers will need to ensure that student data is anonymized, secure, and used only for the purpose of improving educational outcomes.

In conclusion, AI has the potential to revolutionize education in Nigeria by personalizing learning, enhancing teacher effectiveness, and providing students with access to high-quality educational resources. However, to fully realize the benefits of AI in education, there will need to be significant investments in digital infrastructure, teacher training, and data privacy protections. By embracing AI, Nigeria can address some of the most pressing challenges in its education system and ensure that all students, regardless of their background or location, have the opportunity to succeed. As Nigeria continues to develop and modernize, AI can play a key role in building an education system that is more inclusive, equitable, and responsive to the needs of the next generation.

CHAPTER 6
AI for Governance Enhancing Public Services and Accountability

Governance has long been one of the most challenging areas for Nigeria. The country has struggled with issues such as corruption, inefficiency, bureaucratic delays, and lack of transparency in public service delivery. These challenges not only undermine the trust that citizens place in government institutions but also hinder the country's overall development. Poor governance fuels a range of other issues, including slow infrastructure development, weak economic growth, and limited social services. In this context, Artificial Intelligence (AI) offers new possibilities to address many of these governance challenges by improving decision-making processes, increasing accountability, and making public services more efficient and accessible.

A primary way AI can improve governance is by automating and streamlining public services. In Nigeria, many government processes are slow, inefficient, and heavily dependent on manual procedures, which causes delays and frustration for citizens. For example, people frequently experience long waiting times for basic services such as renewing passports, obtaining permits, or registering businesses. AI-powered systems have the potential to transform these services by automating routine tasks and improving their efficiency. This can significantly reduce the time and resources needed to process applications, issue documents, or complete transactions.

For example, AI-powered chatbots and virtual assistants can interact with citizens, helping them access government services online, guiding them through necessary steps, and answering questions in real-time. These automated systems can handle routine inquiries, allowing government employees to focus on more complex and higher-priority issues. Moreover, the automation of these tasks can help standardize the processes, reducing opportunities for human error or manipulation, and thus improving overall service delivery.

In addition to improving the efficiency of public services, AI can enhance the transparency of government operations. Many government processes in Nigeria are opaque, and citizens often lack clear information about how decisions are made, how public funds are allocated, or the progress of government projects. AI-driven data platforms can provide citizens with real-time access to information about budgets, expenditures, public procurement, and project timelines. This kind of transparency can help reduce corruption by making it easier for citizens, civil society organizations, and journalists to monitor how public funds are being used and to hold government officials accountable for any misuse or mismanagement of resources.

Corruption remains one of the most pervasive issues in Nigerian governance, and AI has the potential to play a significant role in combating it. AI systems can automate processes that are traditionally vulnerable to human manipulation, reducing opportunities for corrupt practices. For instance, AI can be used to monitor procurement processes, identifying irregularities or patterns that suggest corruption. AI algorithms can analyze large datasets from public contracts to detect potential conflicts of interest, bid-rigging, or fraudulent transactions. When these algorithms detect anomalies, they can flag them for further investigation, enabling government agencies to take corrective action before public resources are misallocated.

Beyond curbing corruption, AI can significantly improve data-driven decision-making within government agencies. A common challenge facing Nigerian policymakers is the lack of reliable data on which to base decisions. Many government agencies operate with limited or outdated data, making it difficult to develop effective policies or allocate resources efficiently. AI can help solve this problem by analyzing large datasets from various sources, providing policymakers with insights that can inform better decision-making. For example, AI systems can analyze data on population growth, infrastructure needs, health trends, and social services to determine where resources should be allocated to achieve the greatest impact. This capacity to analyze trends, predict future needs, and evaluate the effectiveness of existing policies can enhance the government's ability to deliver services that truly benefit the population.

In the realm of electoral processes, AI has the potential to improve the integrity and efficiency of elections, which have historically been plagued by fraud, irregularities, and violence. AI-powered systems can monitor voting patterns, detect irregularities, and verify the accuracy of voter registration data. For instance, facial recognition technology can be used to ensure that only eligible voters participate in elections, reducing the risk of voter impersonation or multiple voting. Moreover, AI can be employed to monitor social media and other online platforms for signs of election-related misinformation, hate speech, or coordinated attempts to disrupt the democratic process. By identifying these threats early, election officials can take measures to counteract their impact and ensure that elections are conducted fairly and transparently.

Urban planning and infrastructure development are other areas where AI can significantly improve governance. Nigeria's rapid population growth, especially in urban centers, has placed enormous pressure on the country's infrastructure. Roads, public transportation, housing, and waste management systems are often inadequate to meet the needs of the growing population. AI can help cities plan for future growth by analyzing data on population trends, traffic patterns, and environmental conditions. AI-powered traffic management systems, for example, can optimize traffic flow by adjusting traffic signals in real-time based on current conditions, which can reduce congestion and improve mobility. Additionally, AI can be used in the design of smart cities that are more efficient, sustainable, and responsive to the needs of residents. By integrating AI into urban planning processes, Nigerian cities can better manage their growth and provide improved services to their citizens.

Despite its potential, the implementation of AI in governance is not without challenges. One major obstacle is the lack of digital infrastructure in many government agencies. For AI to be effectively implemented, government systems need to be digitized, and data must be collected, stored, and processed in a structured and secure manner. Many government agencies in Nigeria still rely on paper-based systems, which are slow, inefficient, and difficult to integrate with AI technologies. To overcome this challenge, there will need to be significant investments in upgrading the digital infrastructure of government institutions, ensuring they have the tools and resources needed to support AI solutions.

Additionally, there is a shortage of skilled professionals in Nigeria who can design, develop, and manage AI systems. AI is a highly specialized field that requires expertise in data science, machine learning, and software engineering. At present, the number of professionals with these skills in Nigeria is limited, particularly within the public sector. To bridge this gap, the government will need to invest in education and training programs that can develop the next generation of AI experts. Partnerships with universities, private sector companies, and international organizations could help provide training and mentorship for students and professionals interested in AI and data science.

Ethical concerns also need to be considered when implementing AI in governance. AI systems rely heavily on data, and there are risks that these systems could perpetuate biases or violate citizens' privacy if not designed and implemented carefully. For example, AI systems trained on biased data could make decisions that disproportionately affect certain groups of people, reinforcing existing inequalities. Moreover, there is the risk that AI could be used to monitor citizens in ways that infringe on their privacy or civil liberties. To address these ethical concerns, there must be clear regulations and guidelines governing the use of AI in governance. These regulations should ensure that AI systems are used in a transparent, fair, and accountable manner, with safeguards in place to protect citizens' rights.

Despite these challenges, the potential benefits of AI in governance are immense. By improving the efficiency, transparency, and accountability of government processes, AI can help restore trust in public institutions and enhance the quality of governance in Nigeria. Additionally, by reducing corruption, improving decision-making, and streamlining public services, AI can contribute to broader development goals, such as economic growth, social inclusion, and poverty reduction.

In conclusion, AI holds significant promise for improving governance in Nigeria. By automating routine tasks, improving transparency, combating corruption, and enhancing decision-making, AI can help create a more efficient, accountable, and responsive government. However, to fully realize these benefits, Nigeria will need to invest in the necessary infrastructure, develop a skilled workforce, and establish regulatory frameworks that ensure the ethical use of AI. With the right approach, AI can be a powerful tool for transforming governance in Nigeria, helping the country overcome its longstanding challenges and build a more prosperous future for its citizens.

CHAPTER 7
AI for Security and Crime Prevention

Security remains one of the most critical challenges facing Nigeria today. The country grapples with a wide range of security threats, including insurgency, terrorism, banditry, organized crime, cybercrime, and communal conflicts. From the rise of Boko Haram and other militant groups in the northeast to violent clashes between herders and farmers in the central regions, and kidnappings, armed robbery, and cybercrimes in urban areas, Nigeria's security situation is complex and multifaceted. These threats have a destabilizing effect on the nation, undermining development, disrupting daily life, and creating widespread fear and uncertainty among citizens. In recent years, the increase in digital and cyber-related crimes has added another dimension to Nigeria's security concerns, making traditional crime-fighting techniques insufficient.

Artificial Intelligence (AI) offers new opportunities to enhance security and crime prevention efforts in Nigeria. By leveraging AI technologies, law enforcement agencies, security forces, and government bodies can improve their ability to predict, detect, and respond to threats more effectively. AI has the potential to analyze vast amounts of data in real time, offering insights that can improve decision-making, enhance surveillance, identify criminal activities, and protect critical infrastructure. From predictive policing to cybersecurity, AI can revolutionize Nigeria's approach to tackling crime and maintaining public safety.

One of the most promising applications of AI in the security sector is predictive policing, which uses AI algorithms to analyze historical crime data and identify patterns that can help law enforcement predict where crimes are likely to occur. By studying factors such as the types of crimes committed, the locations where they occur, the time of day, and demographic data, AI can help identify crime hotspots. Law enforcement agencies can use this information to allocate resources more efficiently and deploy officers to areas where crimes are most likely to occur. For example, if AI algorithms reveal a pattern of increased burglaries in a specific neighborhood, police patrols can be increased in that area, potentially deterring future incidents. Predictive policing allows law enforcement to be more proactive, focusing on crime prevention rather than merely responding after the fact.

AI can also enhance surveillance capabilities, making it easier for law enforcement agencies to monitor public spaces and detect suspicious behavior in real-time. AI-powered surveillance systems, including facial recognition technology, can identify persons of interest, such as suspects or wanted criminals, in crowded places like airports, shopping malls, or stadiums. These systems compare live footage from surveillance cameras against databases of known criminals or missing persons, alerting authorities when a match is found. Additionally, AI algorithms can analyze video footage to detect unusual or suspicious behavior, such as someone loitering in a high-risk area or acting in ways that may indicate criminal intent. AI-driven surveillance can significantly enhance security efforts in high-risk areas, allowing law enforcement to intervene before a crime is committed.

In the fight against terrorism and insurgency, AI can play a critical role in both detecting threats and disrupting terrorist networks. Nigeria has faced a prolonged battle with Boko Haram in the northeast, as well as rising violence from other militant groups. AI can be used to monitor online activities, including social media, forums, and encrypted messaging apps, to identify individuals or groups who are involved in planning terrorist attacks or recruiting new members. AI systems can analyze vast amounts of data from digital communications, searching for patterns or keywords associated with extremist activity. This can help security forces identify potential threats early, preventing attacks before they occur.

AI's ability to process data quickly and accurately can also be applied to counter-terrorism intelligence gathering, where it can analyze intelligence reports, surveillance footage, and other data sources to provide actionable insights. By analyzing the movements, communications, and associations of known terrorists, AI can help map out terrorist networks, identify key leaders, and track the flow of weapons or financial resources that support terrorist activities. This intelligence can be used to plan targeted operations against terrorist cells, disrupt their supply chains, and weaken their ability to operate.

Cybersecurity is another critical area where AI can enhance Nigeria's security landscape. As Nigeria becomes more digitized, with the rapid growth of its tech and fintech industries, the country has become increasingly vulnerable to cyberattacks. Cybercriminals exploit weak security systems to carry out a variety of crimes, including hacking, phishing, identity theft, and financial fraud. AI-powered cybersecurity tools can help protect government institutions, businesses, and individuals from these threats by detecting and responding to cyberattacks in real time.

AI-based cybersecurity systems can monitor network traffic, detect anomalies, and identify unusual behavior that may indicate a security breach. For example, if an AI system detects a large volume of data being transferred from a government server to an unauthorized location, it can flag the activity for further investigation or automatically shut down the connection to prevent sensitive information from being compromised. AI systems can also be trained to recognize phishing attempts, malware, and other cyber threats, allowing organizations to respond quickly before any significant damage occurs. As cyber threats continue to evolve and become more sophisticated, AI can help Nigeria's cybersecurity infrastructure stay ahead of cybercriminals by continuously learning from new attack patterns and adapting its defenses accordingly.

AI can also play a significant role in improving the criminal justice system by streamlining processes and reducing the backlog of cases that plague Nigerian courts. The legal system in Nigeria is notoriously slow, with many defendants languishing in pretrial detention for years due to delayed court proceedings. AI-powered legal systems can automate certain aspects of the judicial process, such as document analysis, case review, and evidence gathering. For example, AI algorithms can be used to review legal documents, identify relevant case law, and summarize key points, reducing the time it takes for lawyers and judges to prepare for trials. AI can also assist in the management of court schedules and case files, helping to reduce administrative bottlenecks and ensuring that cases move through the system more efficiently.

In addition to improving the efficiency of the legal system, AI can be used to improve the fairness of judicial outcomes by analyzing sentencing patterns to identify and reduce bias. AI systems can analyze data on past sentencing decisions to detect discrepancies or patterns of discrimination, such as harsher penalties for certain demographic groups. By flagging these patterns, AI can help judges and legal professionals make more equitable decisions, ensuring that justice is applied fairly across all segments of society.

Despite the many advantages AI brings to security and crime prevention, its use also raises ethical concerns and risks, particularly regarding privacy and civil liberties. AI-driven surveillance systems, such as facial recognition technology, can be highly invasive, raising questions about how much monitoring is acceptable in a free society. There is a risk that such technologies could be misused by authorities to monitor political opponents, journalists, or activists, infringing on their rights to privacy and freedom of expression. Furthermore, the data used to train AI systems may contain biases that could lead to discriminatory outcomes. For example, if an AI system used for predictive policing is trained on data that reflects historical biases in law enforcement, it may disproportionately target certain racial, ethnic, or socioeconomic groups.

To address these concerns, Nigeria must establish clear regulations and ethical guidelines governing the use of AI in security and crime prevention. These regulations should ensure that AI systems are used in ways that respect individual rights, are free from bias, and are subject to oversight to prevent abuses of power. Transparency will also be crucial; citizens must be informed about how AI is being used in security operations, what data is being collected, and how it is being used to protect their rights and privacy.

Another challenge in deploying AI for security is ensuring that law enforcement agencies and security forces have the technical expertise to effectively use AI technologies. AI systems require ongoing maintenance, updates, and training to ensure they remain effective in the face of evolving threats. Nigerian security agencies will need to invest in building the technical skills of their personnel, providing training in AI, data analysis, and cybersecurity. Partnerships with tech companies, universities, and international organizations could play a key role in developing these capabilities.

In conclusion, AI holds immense potential to enhance security and crime prevention efforts in Nigeria. By enabling predictive policing, improving surveillance, combating terrorism, and strengthening cybersecurity, AI can help law enforcement agencies and security forces respond more effectively to the complex threats facing the country. However, the use of AI in security must be carefully managed to ensure that it respects privacy, avoids discrimination, and operates within a framework of transparency and accountability. With the right investments in infrastructure, expertise, and regulation, AI can play a transformative role in building a safer and more secure Nigeria for all its citizens.

CHAPTER 8
Financial Inclusion and AI in Nigeria's Fintech Revolution

Nigeria's financial landscape has undergone a rapid transformation over the past decade, driven in large part by the rise of financial technology (fintech) companies. These fintech innovations have helped expand access to financial services, particularly for urban populations, and have sparked the development of a vibrant digital economy. However, despite these advances, a significant portion of Nigeria's population remains unbanked or underbanked, particularly in rural areas. Financial inclusion is critical to reducing poverty, fostering economic growth, and empowering citizens to improve their financial well-being.

Artificial Intelligence (AI) offers powerful tools to address the financial inclusion gap in Nigeria, enabling fintech companies and financial institutions to extend their reach to underserved populations, reduce barriers to access, and provide more tailored financial products and services. AI can play a crucial role in helping to break down traditional barriers to financial services, such as limited access to credit, high transaction costs, and complex onboarding processes.

One of the most significant ways AI can contribute to financial inclusion is through improving credit scoring. In the traditional banking system, credit scoring is typically based on a narrow set of data points, such as a borrower's formal credit history, income, and employment status. This approach excludes a large portion of the population who do not have formal financial histories, particularly those working in the informal economy, which represents a substantial share of Nigeria's workforce. AI-powered credit scoring systems, however, can analyze alternative data sources to assess creditworthiness more accurately and inclusively. By analyzing data from mobile phone usage, utility payments, social media activity, and even behavioral patterns, AI can build a more holistic and reliable profile of an individual's financial behavior. This approach allows fintech companies to extend loans and credit services to individuals who would otherwise be excluded from the formal banking sector, giving them the opportunity to invest in businesses, improve their livelihoods, and participate more fully in the economy.

AI can also expand financial access through mobile banking and digital platforms, which have already gained significant traction in Nigeria. With mobile penetration high even in rural areas, mobile-based financial services are crucial for reaching the unbanked. AI-powered mobile banking apps can offer users a range of financial services such as savings accounts, loans, and insurance directly through their smartphones, without the need to visit a physical bank branch. These apps can be designed to be user-friendly, employing natural language processing (NLP) to support local languages and even voice commands, making them accessible to individuals with limited literacy or technical skills. AI chatbots can serve as virtual financial assistants, guiding users through complex transactions, answering questions, and offering personalized advice. These capabilities make digital financial services more accessible, particularly for populations that may be intimidated by traditional banking procedures.

In addition to improving access to financial services, AI can significantly enhance the security of digital financial transactions. Fraud and cybercrime remain major concerns in Nigeria's financial sector, contributing to a lack of trust in digital financial systems. AI-powered fraud detection systems can monitor transactions in real-time, identifying unusual patterns or behavior that may indicate fraudulent activity. For example, if an individual's account is suddenly accessed from multiple locations within a short period, or if large transactions are made outside of typical spending patterns, AI systems can flag the activity for further investigation. In some cases, the system may automatically freeze the account or require additional verification to prevent fraudulent transactions. This real-time monitoring capability allows financial institutions to detect and respond to cyber threats more quickly, reducing the risk of fraud and building trust with customers.

Moreover, AI can help fintech companies develop personalized financial products that meet the unique needs of underserved populations. AI algorithms can analyze customer data to identify patterns in spending, saving, and borrowing behavior, allowing fintech companies to offer customized financial products tailored to individual customers. For example, AI can help identify customers who may benefit from microloans, short-term savings plans, or flexible repayment schedules based on their financial habits. This level of personalization can make financial services more relevant and attractive to customers who may have previously felt alienated by one-size-fits-all financial products.

AI is also revolutionizing the onboarding process for new customers, particularly in meeting Know Your Customer (KYC) and anti-money laundering (AML) requirements. Traditionally, opening a bank account or accessing financial services in Nigeria has required extensive documentation and in-person verification, which can be a major barrier for individuals without formal identification or those living far from bank branches. AI-powered KYC solutions can automate much of the onboarding process by using biometric data, such as facial recognition and fingerprint scanning, to verify identities remotely. AI algorithms can also cross-check documents, such as national ID cards or utility bills, against government databases, allowing users to open accounts or apply for loans without needing to visit a physical location. This streamlined process makes it easier for individuals to access financial services while ensuring that fintech companies remain compliant with regulatory requirements.

In addition to streamlining the onboarding process, AI can improve remittance services, which are a vital source of income for many Nigerian households. Nigeria is one of the largest recipients of remittances in Africa, with billions of dollars sent back to the country each year by Nigerians living abroad. However, the cost of sending remittances through traditional channels can be high, particularly for small transactions. AI-powered platforms can reduce the cost and time of remittances by optimizing transaction routes, eliminating unnecessary intermediaries, and improving exchange rates. This makes remittance services more affordable and accessible to lower-income households, enabling them to receive funds more quickly and securely.

Despite these benefits, there are several challenges to implementing AI for financial inclusion in Nigeria. One of the most significant is the digital divide, particularly in rural areas where access to the internet and smartphones is limited. While mobile penetration is high, many people in remote areas still lack reliable internet access or the digital literacy needed to navigate AI-powered financial platforms effectively. Bridging this gap will require investment in digital infrastructure, including expanding access to high-speed internet in underserved regions and developing affordable devices that enable more people to participate in the digital economy. Additionally, fintech companies and government agencies must invest in financial education programs that help users understand how to use digital financial services safely and effectively.

Another challenge is the need for a robust regulatory framework to govern the use of AI in financial services. The Nigerian financial sector is heavily regulated, and there are concerns about how AI will be integrated into existing regulations, particularly regarding data privacy, consumer protection, and cybersecurity. AI systems rely on large amounts of personal data to function effectively, but this raises questions about how that data is collected, stored, and used. There are also concerns about the potential for AI algorithms to perpetuate biases if not properly designed and tested. For example, if an AI system is trained on biased data, it may make decisions that unfairly exclude certain groups of people from accessing financial services. To address these concerns, regulators will need to establish clear guidelines for the use of AI in financial services, ensuring that these systems are transparent, accountable, and designed to protect consumer rights.

In conclusion, AI has the potential to drive a new wave of financial inclusion in Nigeria, bringing millions of unbanked and underbanked individuals into the formal financial system. By improving credit scoring, expanding mobile banking, enhancing security, and streamlining onboarding processes, AI can help fintech companies and financial institutions extend their reach to underserved populations, offering financial services that are more accessible, personalized, and secure. However, realizing the full potential of AI for financial inclusion will require addressing key challenges, including the digital divide, regulatory concerns, and the need for financial literacy. With the right investments in infrastructure, education, and governance, AI can play a transformative role in fostering financial inclusion and driving economic development in Nigeria.

CHAPTER 9
AI in the Energy Sector Solving Power Challenges

N igeria's energy sector is plagued by persistent challenges that have had a significant impact on the country's economic growth and quality of life. Access to reliable electricity is limited, with frequent power outages and load shedding affecting both urban and rural areas. Many businesses and households rely on expensive generators to meet their energy needs, and the lack of a stable power supply has been a major constraint on industrial development and foreign investment. In addition, energy theft, poor infrastructure, and inefficient management of the national grid have further exacerbated the country's energy crisis. Artificial Intelligence (AI) offers new tools that can help address these challenges by optimizing energy production, improving grid management, and supporting the integration of renewable energy sources.

One of the primary ways AI can improve Nigeria's energy sector is by enhancing the management of the national power grid. The Nigerian power grid is currently inefficient, with significant losses occurring during transmission and distribution. AI-powered grid management systems can help monitor and optimize the flow of electricity in real-time, reducing these losses and improving the overall reliability of the grid. For example, AI algorithms can analyze data from sensors placed throughout the grid to detect faults, identify areas where energy is being lost, and predict potential equipment failures. By identifying and addressing these issues proactively, AI can help reduce downtime and improve the stability of the power supply.

AI can also play a key role in reducing energy theft, which is a major problem in Nigeria. Many consumers bypass meters or tamper with them to avoid paying for electricity, leading to significant revenue losses for power companies. AI-powered monitoring systems can detect patterns of abnormal energy consumption that may indicate theft, allowing power companies to take action before the problem escalates. For example, AI algorithms can analyze data from smart meters to identify discrepancies between the amount of electricity being supplied and the amount being billed. By using AI to detect and prevent energy theft, power companies can improve their revenue collection and invest in further improvements to the grid.

Another area where AI can make a significant impact is in demand forecasting and load balancing. One of the challenges facing Nigeria's energy sector is the mismatch between electricity supply and demand, which often leads to load shedding and power outages. AI can help address this issue by analyzing historical data on energy consumption patterns and predicting future demand with greater accuracy. This allows power companies to plan their production schedules more effectively, ensuring that they generate enough electricity to meet demand without overproducing and wasting resources. AI can also help balance the load on the grid by automatically adjusting the distribution of electricity based on real-time demand, preventing overloads and reducing the need for load shedding.

In addition to optimizing the management of the existing power grid, AI can support the integration of renewable energy sources into Nigeria's energy mix. Nigeria has significant potential for renewable energy, particularly in the form of solar power, but the adoption of renewable energy has been slow due to challenges related to infrastructure, cost, and intermittency. AI can help overcome some of these challenges by optimizing the operation of renewable energy systems. For example, AI-powered systems can predict solar radiation levels and adjust the operation of solar panels to maximize energy production. AI can also be used to manage hybrid energy systems, which combine renewable energy sources with traditional power generation methods, ensuring a stable and reliable power supply even when renewable energy generation is intermittent.

AI can also help improve energy efficiency at the consumer level by enabling smart home and building management systems. These systems use AI algorithms to monitor energy consumption in real-time and automatically adjust heating, cooling, lighting, and other systems to reduce energy waste. For example, a smart home system might use AI to learn the habits of the occupants and adjust the thermostat when they are not home, saving energy without sacrificing comfort. These systems can also provide consumers with detailed insights into their energy usage, helping them identify ways to reduce consumption and lower their electricity bills.

However, while AI offers significant potential to improve Nigeria's energy sector, there are challenges that need to be addressed to fully realize these benefits. One of the main challenges is the lack of digital infrastructure in the energy sector. To implement AI-powered solutions, the national grid, power plants, and distribution networks need to be equipped with sensors, smart meters, and other digital technologies that can collect and transmit data. Currently, much of Nigeria's energy infrastructure is outdated and lacks the necessary digital capabilities to support AI. Significant investments will be required to modernize the infrastructure and ensure that it is capable of integrating AI technologies.

Another challenge is the need for skilled professionals who can design, develop, and manage AI-powered energy systems. The implementation of AI in the energy sector requires expertise in data science, machine learning, and energy management, but there is currently a shortage of professionals with these skills in Nigeria. To address this gap, there will need to be investments in education and training programs that can develop the next generation of energy and AI experts. This could include partnerships with universities, technical schools, and international organizations to provide training and mentorship for students and professionals interested in AI and energy management.

There are also regulatory challenges related to the use of AI in the energy sector. The energy sector in Nigeria is heavily regulated, and there are concerns about how AI will be integrated into existing regulatory frameworks. For example, there are questions about how AI-powered grid management systems will interact with traditional power generation and distribution companies, and how data collected by AI systems will be protected and used. To address these concerns, there will need to be clear regulations governing the use of AI in the energy sector, ensuring that these technologies are implemented in a way that is transparent, accountable, and beneficial to all stakeholders.

In conclusion, AI has the potential to transform Nigeria's energy sector by improving the management of the national grid, reducing energy theft, optimizing demand forecasting, and supporting the integration of renewable energy sources. By leveraging AI, Nigeria can address many of the challenges that have historically constrained its energy sector, improved the reliability and efficiency of the power supply and supported the country's broader economic development goals. However, to fully realize the potential of AI in the energy sector, there will need to be investments in digital infrastructure, education, and regulatory frameworks that ensure these technologies are used in a way that benefits all Nigerians.

CHAPTER 10
Transportation and AI Easing Urban Mobility

Transportation is a critical component of Nigeria's infrastructure, underpinning economic activity and influencing the quality of life for millions of people. Yet, the country faces significant transportation challenges, particularly in its rapidly growing cities. Urban centers like Lagos and Abuja are plagued by severe traffic congestion, inadequate public transportation systems, and poorly maintained roads. These issues not only lead to long commuting times and reduced productivity but also contribute to air pollution, road accidents, and an overall decline in the quality of life for city residents. Artificial Intelligence (AI) has the potential to revolutionize Nigeria's transportation sector by easing congestion, improving public transport, and optimizing traffic management systems.

One of the most pressing challenges in Nigeria's urban centers is traffic congestion, which is exacerbated by the country's rapid urbanization and population growth. Lagos, for instance, is known for its notorious traffic jams, which can cause commuters to spend hours on the road each day. AI can help mitigate this issue by optimizing traffic management systems. Through the use of AI-powered traffic control systems, traffic signals can be adjusted in real-time based on the current flow of vehicles. AI algorithms can analyze data from cameras, sensors, and GPS devices to monitor traffic patterns and predict congestion before it occurs. This enables authorities to manage traffic more efficiently, reducing delays and improving the overall flow of vehicles through the city.

In addition to optimizing traffic signals, AI can also help manage traffic enforcement more effectively. In many Nigerian cities, traffic violations such as running red lights, illegal parking, and reckless driving are common, contributing to traffic accidents and further exacerbating congestion. AI-powered surveillance systems can monitor roadways for traffic violations, using computer vision technology to detect rule-breaking behaviors and automatically issue fines or warnings to offenders. This not only helps improve traffic safety but also reduces the need for manual enforcement by traffic officers, who are often overstretched and unable to cover all areas of the city.

Public transportation is another area where AI can play a transformative role. Nigeria's public transportation systems, particularly in cities like Lagos, are often overcrowded, inefficient, and unreliable. AI-powered solutions can improve the efficiency and reliability of public transport by optimizing routes and schedules based on real-time data. For example, AI algorithms can analyze data on passenger demand, traffic conditions, and vehicle availability to recommend the most efficient routes for buses or taxis.

This can help reduce waiting times for passengers, improve the utilization of public transport vehicles, and ensure that transportation services are more responsive to the needs of the population.

AI can also enhance the customer experience in public transport by providing real-time information on vehicle locations and expected arrival times. In many Nigerian cities, passengers often have little information about when their bus or taxi will arrive, leading to uncertainty and long waiting times. AI-powered apps can track the location of public transport vehicles and provide passengers with accurate, up-to-date information about when their ride will arrive. This can help improve the overall reliability of public transport services and encourage more people to use them, reducing the number of private vehicles on the road and easing congestion.

In addition to improving traffic management and public transportation, AI has the potential to support the development of smart cities in Nigeria. Smart cities leverage data and technology to optimize urban services, making cities more livable, sustainable, and efficient. AI can be used to manage a wide range of urban services, including parking, waste management, and energy consumption. For example, AI-powered parking systems can help drivers find available parking spaces more easily by using sensors to detect vacant spots and directing drivers to them via a mobile app. This can reduce the time drivers spend searching for parking, which is a significant contributor to urban congestion.

AI can also play a role in improving road safety in Nigeria, which has one of the highest rates of road accidents in the world. AI-powered systems can monitor road conditions in real-time, detecting hazards such as potholes, debris, or accidents. By alerting authorities to these hazards, AI can help ensure that roads are maintained more effectively, reducing the risk of accidents. Additionally, AI can be used in vehicles to enhance driver safety through the use of advanced driver-assistance systems (ADAS). These systems use AI to detect potential collisions, alert drivers to dangerous behaviors such as speeding or tailgating, and even take corrective action if necessary, such as automatically applying the brakes to avoid a crash.

Autonomous vehicles, which rely heavily on AI, represent the future of transportation and have the potential to significantly reduce congestion and improve road safety. While fully autonomous vehicles are still in the development stage, AI-powered features such as adaptive cruise control, lane-keeping assistance, and automatic braking are already being integrated into vehicles around the world. In the long term, autonomous vehicles could play a major role in Nigeria's transportation system by reducing the number of human errors that lead to accidents, improving fuel efficiency, and making transportation more accessible for people who are unable to drive.

However, the adoption of AI in Nigeria's transportation sector is not without challenges. One of the main barriers is the lack of adequate infrastructure to support AI-powered solutions. Many roads in

Nigeria are in poor condition, and the country's traffic management systems are often outdated or non-existent. To fully benefit from AI, there will need to be significant investments in upgrading the country's transportation infrastructure, including the installation of sensors, cameras, and other digital technologies that can collect and transmit data in real-time. Additionally, there will need to be investment in public transportation systems to ensure that they are capable of integrating AI-powered solutions and improving their services.

Another challenge is the need for data. AI systems rely on large amounts of data to function effectively, but in many Nigerian cities, data on traffic patterns, road conditions, and public transport usage is either not collected or not available in a structured format. To address this challenge, there will need to be greater efforts to collect, standardize, and share transportation data across different government agencies and private sector actors. This could involve partnerships between the government, private companies, and international organizations to build data-sharing platforms that can support AI-powered solutions.

In addition to these technical challenges, there are also regulatory and ethical considerations related to the use of AI in transportation. For example, there are concerns about how AI-powered surveillance systems will be used and whether they will infringe on citizens' privacy rights. There are also questions about how AI-driven traffic enforcement will be implemented and whether it will be applied fairly across different socioeconomic groups. To address these concerns, there will need to be clear regulations governing the use of AI in transportation, ensuring that these technologies are used in a way that respects citizens' rights and promotes fairness and transparency.

Despite these challenges, the potential benefits of AI in Nigeria's transportation sector are immense. By improving traffic management, enhancing public transportation, and supporting the development of smart cities, AI can help alleviate the transportation challenges that have long plagued Nigeria's urban centers. In doing so, AI can improve the quality of life for millions of Nigerians, reduce the environmental impact of transportation, and support the country's broader economic development goals.

In conclusion, AI offers a powerful set of tools that can help address Nigeria's transportation challenges, from traffic congestion to inadequate public transport systems. By leveraging AI to optimize traffic flow, enhance public transport services, and improve road safety, Nigeria can create more efficient and sustainable urban environments. However, to fully realize the potential of AI in transportation, there will need to be investments in infrastructure, data collection, and regulatory frameworks that ensure these technologies are implemented in a way that benefits all Nigerians. With the right approach, AI can play a key role in transforming Nigeria's transportation system and making the country's cities more livable, productive, and resilient.

CHAPTER 11
AI and the Environment Addressing Nigeria's Environmental Challenges

Nigeria faces significant environmental challenges that threaten both its economy and the well-being of its people. These challenges include deforestation, pollution, desertification, flooding, and the impacts of climate change. The country's rapid population growth, urbanization, and industrialization have put immense pressure on natural resources, leading to environmental degradation. Addressing these challenges is critical for ensuring sustainable development, protecting biodiversity, and mitigating the impacts of climate change. Artificial Intelligence (AI) offers innovative solutions that can help Nigeria tackle its environmental issues by improving environmental monitoring, optimizing resource use, and supporting conservation efforts.

One of the most pressing environmental challenges facing Nigeria is deforestation, which is driven by logging, agriculture, and urban expansion. Deforestation has significant consequences for biodiversity, water resources, and carbon emissions, contributing to climate change and desertification in parts of the country. AI can play a key role in monitoring deforestation and supporting reforestation efforts. AI-powered satellite imagery analysis can track changes in forest cover over time, providing real-time data on deforestation rates. This information can help government agencies and conservation organizations identify areas that are at risk of deforestation and take targeted action to protect these regions. Additionally, AI can be used to monitor the health of reforested areas, ensuring that tree planting efforts are successful and that new forests are growing as expected.

In addition to deforestation, Nigeria faces severe air and water pollution, particularly in urban and industrial areas. Pollution from vehicles, factories, and oil extraction has led to poor air quality, while industrial waste and untreated sewage have contaminated rivers and lakes, affecting both human health and ecosystems. AI can help address these issues by providing real-time monitoring of air and water quality. For example, AI-powered sensors can be deployed in cities to measure air pollution levels, track sources of pollution, and predict pollution spikes based on traffic patterns and weather conditions. Similarly, AI algorithms can analyze data from water sensors to detect contaminants and identify pollution sources in rivers and lakes. By providing real-time data on pollution levels, AI can help policymakers and environmental agencies take timely action to reduce pollution and protect public health.

AI can also support Nigeria's efforts to combat desertification, which is a major problem in the northern regions of the country.

Desertification, driven by unsustainable agricultural practices, overgrazing, and climate change, is leading to the degradation of arable land, threatening food security and livelihoods. AI can help mitigate desertification by optimizing land use and supporting sustainable farming practices. For example, AI-powered precision agriculture systems can provide farmers with data on soil conditions, water availability, and crop health, enabling them to use resources more efficiently and reduce the pressure on the land. Additionally, AI can be used to model the impacts of different land management strategies, helping policymakers develop policies that promote sustainable land use and prevent further desertification.

Climate change is another major environmental challenge facing Nigeria, with rising temperatures, changing rainfall patterns, and more frequent extreme weather events posing risks to agriculture, infrastructure, and public health. AI can help Nigeria adapt to the impacts of climate change by providing data-driven insights into climate patterns and supporting disaster preparedness efforts. For example, AI algorithms can analyze historical climate data to predict future trends in temperature, rainfall, and sea-level rise. This information can help farmers plan their planting and harvesting schedules, enabling them to adapt to changing weather conditions and reduce the risk of crop failure. AI can also support early warning systems for natural disasters such as floods and droughts, providing real-time alerts that allow communities to prepare and respond more effectively.

In addition to addressing the immediate impacts of climate change, AI can also support efforts to reduce greenhouse gas emissions and promote the transition to renewable energy. Nigeria has significant potential for renewable energy, particularly in the form of solar power, but the adoption of renewable energy has been slow due to challenges related to cost, infrastructure, and intermittency. AI can help overcome some of these challenges by optimizing the operation of renewable energy systems. For example, AI-powered energy management systems can predict energy demand and adjust the operation of solar panels or wind turbines to maximize energy production and minimize waste. AI can also be used to integrate renewable energy into the national grid, ensuring a stable and reliable power supply even when renewable energy generation is intermittent.

Another area where AI can make a significant impact is in waste management, which is a growing problem in Nigeria's urban centers. Many cities struggle with inadequate waste collection and disposal systems, leading to the accumulation of garbage in streets, waterways, and public spaces. AI-powered waste management systems can improve the efficiency of waste collection by analyzing data on waste generation patterns and optimizing collection routes. These systems can also support recycling efforts by using AI algorithms to sort waste materials more effectively, ensuring that recyclable materials are separated from non-recyclable waste. By improving waste management, AI can help reduce pollution, protect public health, and promote a more sustainable urban environment.

Despite the potential benefits of AI in addressing Nigeria's environmental challenges, there are also obstacles to its widespread adoption. One of the main challenges is the lack of digital infrastructure in many parts of the country, particularly in rural areas where environmental degradation is most severe. To implement AI-powered solutions, there will need to be investments in sensors, data collection platforms, and communication networks that can transmit environmental data in real-time. Additionally, there is a need for more collaboration between government agencies, research institutions, and private companies to ensure that AI technologies are developed and deployed in a way that addresses Nigeria's specific environmental needs.

Another challenge is the need for environmental data. AI systems rely on large amounts of data to function effectively, but in many cases, data on environmental conditions in Nigeria is either not available or not collected in a structured format. To address this issue, there will need to be greater efforts to collect, standardize, and share environmental data across different government agencies, research institutions, and conservation organizations. This could involve the development of national or regional databases that provide access to real-time data on deforestation, air and water quality, climate patterns, and other environmental indicators.

In conclusion, AI has the potential to play a transformative role in addressing Nigeria's environmental challenges by improving environmental monitoring, optimizing resource use, and supporting conservation efforts. By leveraging AI to monitor deforestation, combat pollution, mitigate desertification, and adapt to climate change, Nigeria can protect its natural resources and ensure a more sustainable future for its people. However, to fully realize the potential of AI in the environmental sector, there will need to be investments in digital infrastructure, data collection, and regulatory frameworks that ensure these technologies are used in a way that benefits both people and the planet. With the right approach, AI can help Nigeria tackle its most pressing environmental challenges and create a more resilient, sustainable, and prosperous future.

CHAPTER 12
AI for Small and Medium Enterprises (SMEs) Driving Economic Growth

Small and Medium Enterprises (SMEs) play a vital role in Nigeria's economy, accounting for a significant portion of employment and contributing to the nation's overall economic development. However, despite their importance, Nigerian SMEs face a number of challenges, including limited access to finance, poor infrastructure, inadequate market opportunities, and operational inefficiencies. Many SMEs struggle to scale their businesses, hampered by a lack of resources, expertise, and technological capabilities. Artificial Intelligence (AI) can help address these challenges by offering tools that can drive growth, improve efficiency, and enable Nigerian SMEs to compete in the global marketplace.

One of the most significant challenges faced by SMEs in Nigeria is access to finance. Traditional banks often require extensive credit histories and collateral, which many small business owners do not have, particularly those operating in the informal sector. AI offers a solution to this challenge by enabling alternative credit scoring models. Instead of relying solely on traditional financial data, AI algorithms can analyze alternative data sources, such as transaction histories, mobile phone usage, and social media activity, to assess the creditworthiness of SME owners. By incorporating these alternative data points, AI can provide a more accurate and inclusive assessment of risk, enabling financial institutions to extend credit to businesses that would otherwise be excluded from the formal financial system.

In addition to improving access to finance, AI can help SMEs streamline their operations and reduce costs. Many small businesses struggle with inefficient processes, which can lead to wasted time and resources. AI-powered automation tools can help address this issue by automating routine tasks such as accounting, inventory management, customer service, and marketing. For example, AI-powered chatbots can handle customer inquiries, freeing up time for business owners to focus on more strategic tasks. Similarly, AI-driven accounting platforms can automatically categorize expenses, generate financial reports, and ensure that businesses remain compliant with tax regulations, reducing the administrative burden on small business owners.

AI can also enhance SMEs' ability to analyze market trends and customer behavior, providing them with valuable insights that can inform business decisions. Many small businesses lack the resources to conduct extensive market research or analyze customer data, which can put them at a disadvantage when competing with larger companies. AI-powered analytics platforms can help level the playing field by providing SMEs with access to data-driven insights. For example, AI algorithms can analyze customer purchasing patterns, social media interactions, and website traffic to identify trends and preferences. This information can help business owners make more informed decisions about product development, pricing, and marketing strategies, ensuring that they are better positioned to meet the needs of their customers.

Marketing is another area where AI can significantly benefit SMEs. Many small businesses struggle to reach their target audiences due to limited marketing budgets and expertise. AI-powered marketing tools can help SMEs optimize their marketing campaigns by analyzing data on customer demographics, preferences, and online behavior. These tools can automatically generate personalized marketing content, such as targeted advertisements, email campaigns, and social media posts, ensuring that businesses reach the right customers with the right messages. By using AI to personalize marketing efforts, SMEs can improve customer engagement, increase sales, and reduce the cost of acquiring new customers.

AI can also play a role in helping SMEs expand their reach beyond local markets and tap into global opportunities. In today's digital economy, businesses no longer need to be limited by geography, and AI can help SMEs overcome the barriers to international expansion. AI-powered translation tools, for instance, can enable SMEs to communicate with customers and partners in different languages, opening up new markets for their products and services. AI can also help SMEs navigate the complexities of international trade by analyzing data on global supply chains, shipping costs, and tariffs, enabling business owners to make informed decisions about where and how to expand their operations.

Supply chain management is another critical area where AI can help SMEs improve their efficiency and competitiveness. Managing supply chains can be particularly challenging for small businesses, as they often lack the resources and expertise to optimize logistics and inventory management. AI-powered supply chain platforms can help SMEs predict demand, manage inventory levels, and identify the most efficient shipping routes. For example, AI algorithms can analyze historical sales data and external factors such as weather patterns and economic conditions to forecast demand more accurately, helping businesses avoid overstocking or understocking their products. By optimizing supply chain operations, SMEs can reduce costs, improve customer satisfaction, and increase profitability.

One of the most promising aspects of AI for SMEs is its ability to democratize access to advanced technologies. Traditionally, AI has been associated with large corporations that have the financial resources to invest in expensive AI solutions and data scientists. However, the rise of AI-as-a-Service (AIaaS) platforms has made AI more accessible to small businesses. These platforms offer a range of AI-powered tools and services on a subscription basis, allowing

SMEs to take advantage of AI without needing to develop their own in-house capabilities. For example, AIaaS platforms can provide businesses with access to machine learning algorithms, natural language processing tools, and computer vision systems, enabling SMEs to incorporate AI into their operations at a fraction of the cost.

Despite the potential benefits of AI for SMEs, there are also challenges that need to be addressed to ensure that small businesses can fully harness the power of AI. One of the main challenges is the lack of digital literacy and technical expertise among many SME owners. While AI offers powerful tools for business growth, many small business owners may not have the skills or knowledge to implement AI solutions effectively. To address this issue, there will need to be greater efforts to provide training and support for SME owners, helping them understand how AI can benefit their businesses and how to integrate AI technologies into their operations.

Another challenge is the need for reliable digital infrastructure. Many SMEs in Nigeria, particularly those in rural areas, do not have access to high-speed internet, which is essential for using AI-powered tools. Without adequate connectivity, businesses may struggle to take full advantage of AI solutions. To overcome this barrier, there will need to be investments in expanding digital infrastructure, particularly in underserved regions, to ensure that all SMEs have the opportunity to leverage AI technologies.

There are also concerns about data privacy and security, particularly as AI relies on large amounts of data to function effectively. SMEs that use AI-powered tools to collect and analyze customer data must ensure that they are complying with data protection regulations and that their customers' information is being handled securely. There is a risk that if AI systems are not implemented with proper safeguards, they could expose businesses to data breaches or misuse of personal information. To address these concerns, SME owners will need to be educated about best practices for data privacy and security, and AI solution providers will need to ensure that their platforms include robust security features.

In conclusion, AI has the potential to transform the SME sector in Nigeria by providing small businesses with the tools they need to grow, improve efficiency, and compete on a global scale. From alternative credit scoring models that improve access to finance, to AI-powered analytics that inform business decisions, AI can help SMEs overcome the challenges that have traditionally limited their growth. However, to fully realize the potential of AI for SMEs, there will need to be investments in digital literacy, infrastructure, and data security. With the right support, AI can empower Nigeria's small business owners to innovate, expand, and drive economic growth, contributing to the country's broader development goals.

CHAPTER 13
The Role of AI in Solving Nigeria's Unemployment Crisis

Unemployment, particularly among Nigeria's youth, is one of the country's most pressing challenges. Nigeria has a young and rapidly growing population, with millions of new entrants joining the labor market each year. However, the country's economy has struggled to create enough jobs to absorb this growing workforce, leading to high levels of unemployment and underemployment. The unemployment crisis has significant social and economic implications, contributing to poverty, insecurity, and political instability. Artificial Intelligence (AI) offers both opportunities and challenges in addressing Nigeria's unemployment crisis. While AI has the potential to create new job opportunities and drive economic growth, it also raises concerns about job displacement and the future of work in an increasingly automated world.

One of the ways AI can help address Nigeria's unemployment crisis is by creating new job opportunities in the technology sector. As AI continues to evolve, there is growing demand for skilled professionals who can develop, implement, and manage AI systems. This includes roles such as data scientists, machine learning engineers, AI researchers, and software developers. By investing in education and training programs that focus on AI and data science, Nigeria can equip its youth with the skills needed to take advantage of these emerging job opportunities. These programs can be offered through universities, technical schools, and online platforms, ensuring that young people across the country have access to the training they need to succeed in the digital economy.

In addition to creating jobs in the AI sector itself, AI can also support job creation in other industries by improving productivity and enabling businesses to scale more effectively. For example, AI-powered tools can help businesses in agriculture, manufacturing, healthcare, and retail optimize their operations, reduce costs, and expand their markets. This, in turn, can lead to the creation of new jobs in these sectors as businesses grow and hire more workers. AI can also support entrepreneurship by providing small business owners with the tools they need to innovate and compete in the marketplace. By enabling businesses to operate more efficiently and reach new customers, AI can help stimulate job creation across a range of industries.

Another area where AI can have a positive impact on employment is in vocational training and skills development. Many young people in Nigeria lack the skills needed to compete in the modern job market, particularly in industries that require technical expertise. AI-powered training platforms can help address this skills gap by providing personalized learning experiences that are tailored to the needs of individual learners. For example, AI algorithms can analyze a learner's progress and recommend specific courses or training modules that will help them develop the skills they need to succeed in their chosen field. These platforms can also use virtual reality (VR) and augmented reality (AR) technologies to provide hands-on training in industries such as manufacturing, construction, and healthcare, enabling learners to gain practical experience in a safe and controlled environment.

AI can also support job matching and recruitment efforts, helping connect job seekers with employers more effectively. Traditional recruitment processes can be time-consuming and inefficient, with employers often struggling to find candidates with the right skills and experience. AI-powered job matching platforms can streamline this process by analyzing data on job seekers' skills, experience, and preferences and matching them with job opportunities that align with their qualifications. These platforms can also use AI to predict which candidates are most likely to succeed in a given role, improving the overall efficiency of the recruitment process. By making it easier for job seekers to find suitable employment and for employers to find qualified candidates, AI can help reduce unemployment and underemployment in Nigeria.

However, while AI offers opportunities for job creation and skills development, there are also concerns about the potential for job displacement as a result of automation. AI-powered automation is already being used to replace human workers in certain tasks, particularly in industries such as manufacturing, logistics, and customer service. For example, AI-powered robots can perform repetitive tasks on assembly lines, while AI chatbots can handle customer inquiries, reducing the need for human workers. This raises concerns about the future of work, particularly for low-skilled workers who may be at risk of losing their jobs to automation.

To address these concerns, it will be important for Nigeria to develop policies that ensure a smooth transition to an AI-driven economy. This could include providing retraining and upskilling programs for workers who are displaced by automation, ensuring that they have the opportunity to transition into new roles that require more advanced skills. Governments and businesses can also work together to develop strategies for integrating AI into the workforce in a way that complements human workers, rather than replacing them. For example, AI can be used to automate routine tasks, allowing workers to focus on more complex and creative aspects of their jobs. By adopting a collaborative approach to AI, Nigeria can ensure that automation leads to job creation rather than job loss.

In addition to addressing the potential for job displacement, there will also need to be efforts to ensure that the benefits of AI are distributed equitably across society. There is a risk that AI could exacerbate existing inequalities if certain groups are excluded from the opportunities created by AI-driven economic growth. For example, individuals in rural areas or those with limited access to education and technology may be left behind in an AI-driven economy. To address this issue, there will need to be targeted efforts to ensure that all Nigerians have access to the education, training, and resources they need to participate in the AI-driven workforce. This could include expanding access to digital infrastructure, providing scholarships or financial assistance for AI training programs, and supporting initiatives that promote diversity and inclusion in the technology sector.

In conclusion, AI has the potential to play a significant role in addressing Nigeria's unemployment crisis by creating new job opportunities, supporting skills development, and improving the efficiency of job matching and recruitment processes. However, to fully realize the potential of AI for job creation, there will need to be investments in education and training, as well as policies that ensure a fair and inclusive transition to an AI-driven economy. By adopting a forward-thinking approach to AI, Nigeria can harness the power of technology to create a more prosperous and equitable future for its people, ensuring that all Nigerians have the opportunity to succeed in the digital economy.

CHAPTER 14
Ethics, Policy, and Regulation AI in Nigeria

As Nigeria embarks on its journey to harness the transformative power of Artificial Intelligence (AI), it is essential to establish a robust ethical framework, policy guidelines, and regulatory mechanisms that ensure AI is used responsibly and for the benefit of all Nigerians. While AI offers significant opportunities to address the country's challenges, it also raises important ethical, social, and legal questions. Issues such as data privacy, algorithmic bias, job displacement, and accountability must be carefully considered to ensure that AI technologies are implemented in a way that promotes fairness, transparency, and respect for human rights.

One of the key ethical concerns related to AI is the issue of data privacy. AI systems rely on vast amounts of data to function effectively, but this raises questions about how personal data is collected, stored, and used. In Nigeria, there is currently limited awareness of data privacy issues, and many individuals are not fully informed about how their personal information is being used by AI-powered platforms. To address this, there will need to be clear regulations governing the collection and use of personal data. This includes ensuring that individuals have control over their own data, that data is collected with their informed consent, and that it is used in a way that respects their privacy. Nigeria's Data Protection Regulation (NDPR), introduced in 2019, is a step in the right direction, but further efforts will be needed to ensure that it is effectively enforced and that it keeps pace with the rapid development of AI technologies.

Another ethical concern is the risk of algorithmic bias. AI systems are only as good as the data they are trained on, and if this data is biased or unrepresentative, the AI system may make decisions that disproportionately affect certain groups of people. For example, if an AI system used for credit scoring is trained on biased data, it may unfairly deny loans to individuals from certain ethnic or socioeconomic backgrounds. Similarly, AI-powered recruitment systems may inadvertently favor certain candidates based on gender, age, or other characteristics. To mitigate these risks, it will be essential to ensure that AI systems are designed and trained in a way that is fair and unbiased. This includes using diverse and representative datasets, conducting regular audits of AI systems, and ensuring that there is transparency in how AI decisions are made.

The issue of accountability is also critical when it comes to the use of AI in decision-making processes. AI systems are increasingly being used to make decisions in areas such as healthcare, finance, and law enforcement, where the consequences of incorrect or biased decisions can be significant. However, AI systems are often seen as "black boxes," where the decision-making process is opaque and difficult to understand. This raises questions about who is accountable when an AI system makes a mistake or produces unfair outcomes. To address this, there will need to be mechanisms in place to ensure that AI systems are transparent and that there is accountability for their decisions. This could include requiring AI developers and users to provide explanations for how AI decisions are made and ensuring that there is a clear chain of responsibility when things go wrong.

The potential for job displacement due to AI-driven automation is another important ethical and social concern. As AI systems become more capable of performing tasks that were previously done by humans, there is a risk that certain jobs, particularly those that are routine or low-skilled, may be replaced by machines. This could lead to significant job losses, particularly in sectors such as manufacturing, logistics, and customer service. To address this issue, there will need to be policies in place to support workers who are displaced by automation, including retraining and upskilling programs that help individuals transition into new roles. Governments and businesses will also need to work together to ensure that the benefits of AI-driven productivity gains are shared across society, rather than concentrated in the hands of a few.

In addition to these ethical concerns, there is also a need for clear policy guidelines and regulatory frameworks that govern the use of AI in Nigeria. While AI has the potential to drive economic growth and improve public services, it is important that its development is guided by a vision that prioritizes social good and respects human rights. This will require collaboration between government, the private sector, civil society, and academia to develop policies that ensure AI is used responsibly and for the benefit of all Nigerians.

One of the key areas where policy is needed is in the regulation of AI in critical sectors such as healthcare, finance, and law enforcement. AI is already being used in these sectors to make decisions that have a direct impact on people's lives, such as diagnosing diseases, approving loans, or predicting criminal behavior. To ensure that AI is used ethically and responsibly in these sectors, there will need to be sector-specific regulations that address issues such as data privacy, bias, and accountability. These regulations should be developed in consultation with stakeholders from across society, including industry experts, human rights advocates, and the communities that will be affected by AI technologies.

There is also a need for Nigeria to develop a national AI strategy that outlines the country's vision for AI development and use. This strategy should set out the government's priorities for AI, including how it plans to support innovation and research, build AI capacity, and address the ethical and social challenges associated with AI. The strategy should also include measures to promote collaboration between the public and private sectors, as well as international partnerships that can help Nigeria access global AI expertise and resources.

In conclusion, while AI offers significant opportunities for Nigeria, it also raises important ethical, social, and legal questions that must be addressed through thoughtful policy and regulation. By developing a robust ethical framework and regulatory mechanisms, Nigeria can ensure that AI is used in a way that promotes fairness, transparency, and respect for human rights. This will be critical to building public trust in AI technologies and ensuring that the benefits of AI are shared across all segments of society. With the right policies in place, AI can be a powerful tool for driving economic growth, improving public services, and creating a more equitable and inclusive future for Nigeria.

CHAPTER 15
The Future of AI in Nigeria Opportunities and Challenges

As Nigeria continues to embrace the transformative potential of Artificial Intelligence (AI), it stands on the cusp of a technological revolution that could reshape the country's economy, governance, and society. AI offers immense opportunities to solve some of Nigeria's most pressing challenges, from improving healthcare and education to enhancing public services and addressing security threats. However, realizing the full potential of AI will require overcoming significant challenges, including the need for infrastructure development, investment in human capital, and the creation of an enabling environment for innovation.

One of the most promising opportunities for AI in Nigeria is its potential to drive economic growth and job creation. As AI technologies become more integrated into various sectors, they can help increase productivity, improve efficiency, and create new industries. For example, AI-powered automation can streamline manufacturing processes, reducing costs and enabling Nigerian companies to compete more effectively in the global marketplace. AI can also drive innovation in agriculture, healthcare, education, and finance, creating new opportunities for entrepreneurship and job creation. However, to fully capitalize on these opportunities, Nigeria will need to invest in education and skills development to ensure that its workforce is prepared for the jobs of the future.

Education and human capital development will be critical to Nigeria's success in the AI-driven economy. As AI continues to evolve, there will be growing demand for professionals with expertise in AI, data science, machine learning, and other related fields. Nigeria's universities and technical schools will need to expand their programs in these areas, and partnerships with international institutions can help accelerate the development of local talent. Additionally, there will need to be efforts to ensure that AI education and training programs are accessible to all Nigerians, regardless of their socioeconomic background or geographic location. By investing in human capital, Nigeria can build a workforce that is capable of driving AI innovation and ensuring that the benefits of AI are shared across society.

Infrastructure development is another critical area where Nigeria will need to focus in order to fully realize the potential of AI. AI systems rely on access to high-quality data, reliable internet connectivity, and advanced computing infrastructure. However, many parts of Nigeria still lack the digital infrastructure needed to support AI technologies, particularly in rural areas. Expanding access to high-speed internet and building data centers and cloud computing infrastructure will be essential to supporting the growth of AI in Nigeria. Additionally, investments in energy infrastructure will be necessary to ensure that AI-powered systems can operate reliably, particularly in regions where electricity supply is inconsistent.

In addition to addressing the technical and infrastructure challenges, Nigeria will also need to create an enabling environment for AI innovation. This includes developing policies and regulations that support the growth of the AI industry while ensuring that AI technologies are used responsibly and ethically. The government will play a key role in fostering innovation by providing funding for AI research and development, supporting startups, and creating incentives for private sector investment in AI. Collaboration between government, the private sector, academia, and civil society will be essential to building a thriving AI ecosystem that can drive sustainable economic growth and improve the quality of life for all Nigerians.

While the future of AI in Nigeria is full of promise, there are also challenges that must be addressed to ensure that the benefits of AI are distributed equitably. One of the risks associated with AI is the potential for increased inequality, as certain segments of the population may be better positioned to take advantage of AI-driven economic opportunities than others. For example, individuals with access to education and technology may benefit more from AI than those in rural or underserved areas. To address this risk, there will need to be targeted efforts to ensure that all Nigerians have access to the tools and resources they need to participate in the AI-driven economy. This could include expanding access to digital infrastructure, providing financial support for AI training programs, and promoting diversity and inclusion in the technology sector.

In conclusion, the future of AI in Nigeria presents both significant opportunities and challenges. By embracing AI, Nigeria can drive economic growth, improve public services, and address some of its most pressing challenges. However, realizing the full potential of AI will require investments in education, infrastructure, and innovation, as well as a commitment to ensuring that AI technologies are used in a way that promotes fairness, transparency, and inclusivity. With the right approach, Nigeria can position itself as a leader in AI innovation in Africa, creating a more prosperous, equitable, and sustainable future for its people.